Ella los cura

por P.A. Schnitzler

Scott Foresman
is an imprint of

Glenview, Illinois • Boston, Massachusetts • Chandler, Arizona
Upper Saddle River, New Jersey

Every effort has been made to secure permission and provide appropriate credit for photographic material. The publisher deeply regrets any omission and pledges to correct errors called to its attention in subsequent editions.

Unless otherwise acknowledged, all photographs are the property of Pearson.

Photo locations denoted as follows: Top (T), Center (C), Bottom (B), Left (L), Right (R), Background (Bkgd)

Opener © Comstock Inc.; 1 © Dorling Kindersley; 3 © Dorling Kindersley; 4 © Dorling Kindersley; 6 (TL) © Dorling Kindersley; 6 (B) © Dorling Kindersley; 7 © Dorling Kindersley; 8 © Comstock

ISBN 13: 978-0-328-53286-5
ISBN 10:   0-328-53286-X

Copyright © by Pearson Education, Inc., or its affiliates. All rights reserved. Printed in the United States of America. This publication is protected by copyright, and permission should be obtained from the publisher prior to any prohibited reproduction, storage in a retrieval system, or transmission in any form or by any means, electronic, mechanical, photocopying, recording, or likewise. For information regarding permissions, write to Pearson Curriculum Rights & Permissions, One Lake Street, Upper Saddle River, New Jersey 07458.

Pearson® is a trademark, in the U.S. and/or other countries, of Pearson plc or its affiliates.

Scott Foresman® is a trademark, in the U.S. and/or other countries, of Pearson Education, Inc., or its affiliates.

2 3 4 5 6 7 8 9 10 V0N4 13 12 11 10

Luci estaba mal.

No se sentía bien.

Leo estaba mal.

No se sentía bien.

Lalo estaba mal.

No se sentía bien.

La veterinaria los examinó.
Ella los curó.

Luis carga a Lalo.

Lo lleva a su casa.

Los veterinarios

Los veterinarios son médicos que examinan y curan a los animales. Estudian las ciencias y cómo son los animales. Para ser veterinario, hay que estudiar muchos años en una universidad. ¡En los Estados Unidos hay miles de veterinarios!